The Marvelous Mojito Cookbook

Many Mouthwatering Mojito Recipes That You Truly Need

Table of Contents

Introduction

Welcome to the wonderful and delicious world of mojitos! This perfect drink has deep roots in Cuban culture but, luckily, it was just too delicious to remain on the island- everyone in the world needed a great mojito! Yet the recipe was first perfected in Havana, Cuba where the discovery was made that white rum, sugar, mint, lime and club soda make an amazingly refreshing drink. The main components of almost every mojito remain the same and why would you need to mess with perfection- this drink has it all! Refreshing mint, sour lime, sweet sugar, bubbly soda and the wonderful addition of rum to top it all off.

While almost everyone loves a good mojito, I have become a true mojito connoisseur over the years and I wanted to share some of the recipes I love with you. No one should ever drink a mojito alone so now everyone can create this great drink! Each recipe in this book is written to serve one person. However, you can easily double, triple or even make the recipe times ten to have a massive pitcher of the drink. Keep in mind that mojitos are best when enjoyed immediately after they are made so that the soda does not go flat. You can choose to muddle all the ingredients together ahead of time and save the soda and ice for the last minute though. Yet once that glass is poured, drink up! I promise you will enjoy it.

Each recipe in this book will bring a new life to a classic drink. You can start with a simple citrus mojito which incorporates oranges and lemons into the mix or opt for something that is a little more diverse like the chocolate mojito (yes, chocolate and mint are fantastic together!). The basil mojito eliminates the mint and replaces it with a more earthy herb while the grilled pineapple mojito will have you loving the sweet taste of caramel. There really is just so much to explore within these pages that I recommend starting on the first page and drinking your way through the book! As always, drink responsibly and enjoy every sip!

Now, go grab that muddler and start mixing up some fresh mojitos!

The Classic Mojito

This recipe makes one, perfect, authentic mojito that tastes exactly how a real mojito should. If you want something truly refreshing that will quench your desire for a mojito, this is the recipe you should start with!

Active Time: 5 minutes

Cooking Time: 0 Minutes

Yield: 1 glass

Ingredients:

- 10 mint leaves, fresh
- 5 teaspoons granulated sugar
- 1 ½ ounces of your favorite white rum
- ½ large lime
- ½ cup fresh club soda (still bubbly)
- Ice

Directions:

1. Cut the half of lime into wedges and place them into a strong glass.

2. Add the fresh mint leaves and the sugar to the glass as well and use a cocktail muddler or wooden spoon to smash the mint together with the sugar and limes. This process helps the mint leaves and the lime to release their natural oils and juices.

3. Add about half a cup of ice cubes to the glass and then pour the white rum over the top. Stir the mix briefly to mix the rum into the minty lime mix and also to help dissolve the sugar.

4. Add the club soda to the drink and stir once to mix everything together. You do not want to stir too much or the carbonation will come out of the soda.

5. Garnish with any extra lime slices and then enjoy!

Brown Sugar Mojito

If you love classic mojitos but want something that is just slightly different and a little bit richer, then you need a brown sugar mojito. The simple addition of dark brown sugar adds a whole new level of flavor to this drink that you are sure to love.

Active Time: 5 minutes

Cooking Time: 0 Minutes

Yield: 1 glass

Ingredients:

- 10 mint leaves, fresh
- 4 tsp dark brown sugar
- 1 ½ ounces of your favorite white rum
- ½ large lime
- ½ cup fresh club soda (still bubbly)
- Ice

Directions:

1. Cut the half of lime into wedges and place them into a strong glass.

2. Add the fresh mint leaves and the brown sugar to the glass as well and use a cocktail muddler or wooden spoon to smash the mint together with the sugar and limes. This process helps the mint leaves and the lime to release their natural oils and juices.

3. Add about half a cup of ice cubes to the glass and then pour the white rum over the top. Stir the mix briefly to mix the rum into the minty lime mix and also to help dissolve the sugar.

4. Add the club soda to the drink and stir once to mix everything together. You do not want to stir too much or the carbonation will come out of the soda.

5. Garnish with any extra lime slices and then enjoy!

The Dark Mojito

Do you love rich drinks with lots of flavor? Then the dark mojito is the drink for you. Rich yet refreshing, minty yet deep, this drink has it all! Perfect for a cold summer night.

Active Time: 5 minutes

Cooking Time: 0 Minutes

Yield: 1 glass

Ingredients:

- 10 mint leaves, fresh
- 4 tsp brown sugar

- 1 ½ ounces of your favorite dark rum
- ½ large lime
- ½ cup fresh club soda (still bubbly)
- Ice

Directions:

1. Cut the half of lime into wedges and place them into a strong glass.

2. Add the fresh mint leaves and the brown sugar to the glass as well and use a cocktail muddler or wooden spoon to smash the mint together with the sugar and limes. This process helps the mint leaves and the lime to release their natural oils and juices.

3. Add about half a cup of ice cubes to the glass and then pour the white rum over the top. Stir the mix briefly to mix the rum into the minty lime mix and also to help dissolve the sugar.

4. Add the club soda to the drink and stir once to mix everything together. You do not want to stir too much or the carbonation will come out of the soda.

5. Garnish with any extra lime slices and then enjoy!

Raspberry Mojito

Raspberries are a natural fit with limes and also with mint. That is why they are perfect with mojitos! Use fresh raspberries whenever possible but frozen can work well too!

Active Time: 5 minutes

Cooking Time: 0 Minutes

Yield: 1 glass

Ingredients:

- 10 mint leaves, fresh
- 5 teaspoons granulated sugar
- 1 ½ ounces of your favorite white rum
- ½ large lime
- ½ cup fresh club soda (still bubbly)
- ½ cup fresh raspberries
- Ice

Directions:

1. Cut the half of lime into wedges and place them into a strong glass.

2. Add the fresh mint leaves, raspberries and the sugar to the glass as well and use a cocktail muddler or wooden spoon to smash the mint together with the sugar and limes. This process helps the mint leaves, raspberries and the lime to release their natural oils and juices.

3. Add about half a cup of ice cubes to the glass and then pour the white rum over the top. Stir the mix briefly to mix

the rum into the minty lime mix and also to help dissolve the sugar.

4. Add the club soda to the drink and stir once to mix everything together. You do not want to stir too much or the carbonation will come out of the soda.

5. Garnish with any extra lime slices and then enjoy!

Strawberry Mojito

Strawberry and mint is one of the most refreshing flavor profiles of summer. Add in fresh lime juice and you have a total win! This drink is like enjoying summer in a glass!

Active Time: 5 minutes

Cooking Time: 0 Minutes

Yield: 1 glass

Ingredients:

- 10 mint leaves, fresh
- 5 teaspoons granulated sugar
- 1 ½ ounces of your favorite white rum

- ½ large lime
- ½ cup fresh club soda (still bubbly)
- ½ cup fresh chopped strawberries
- Ice

Directions:

1. Cut the half of lime into wedges and place them into a strong glass.

2. Add the fresh mint leaves, chopped strawberries and the sugar to the glass as well and use a cocktail muddler or wooden spoon to smash the mint together with the sugar and limes. This process helps the mint leaves, strawberries and the lime to release their natural oils and juices.

3. Add about half a cup of ice cubes to the glass and then pour the white rum over the top. Stir the mix briefly to mix the rum into the minty lime mix and also to help dissolve the sugar.

4. Add the club soda to the drink and stir once to mix everything together. You do not want to stir too much or the carbonation will come out of the soda.

5. Garnish with any extra lime slices and then enjoy!

Blueberry Mojito

This mojito is definitely not the most beautiful on the block (mashing blueberries can make a grayish color) but the abundant flavor more than makes up for it. Opt for fresh blueberries to ensure the most flavor possible.

Active Time: 5 minutes

Cooking Time: 0 Minutes

Yield: 1 glass

Ingredients:

- 10 mint leaves, fresh
- 5 teaspoons granulated sugar
- 1 ½ ounces of your favorite white rum
- ½ large lime
- ½ cup fresh club soda (still bubbly)
- ½ cup fresh blueberries
- Ice

Directions:

1. Cut the half of lime into wedges and place them into a strong glass.

2. Add the fresh mint leaves, blueberries and the sugar to the glass as well and use a cocktail muddler or wooden spoon to smash the mint together with the sugar and limes. This process helps the mint leaves, blueberries and the lime to release their natural oils and juices.

3. Add about half a cup of ice cubes to the glass and then pour the white rum over the top. Stir the mix briefly to mix the rum into the minty lime mix and also to help dissolve the sugar.

4. Add the club soda to the drink and stir once to mix everything together. You do not want to stir too much or the carbonation will come out of the soda.

5. Garnish with any extra lime slices and then enjoy!

Mixed Berry Mojito

Summer is all about fresh berries and bright flavors and that is the perfect description of this drink. Enjoy this mojito on a hot summer's day when you need something refreshing that uses all those beautiful berries you have on hand.

Active Time: 5 minutes

Cooking Time: 0 Minutes

Yield: 1 glass

Ingredients:

- 10 mint leaves, fresh
- 5 teaspoons granulated sugar
- 1 ½ ounces of your favorite white rum
- ½ large lime
- ½ cup fresh club soda (still bubbly)
- 5 fresh raspberries
- 10 fresh blueberries
- ¼ cup fresh chopped strawberries
- Ice

Directions:

1. Cut the half of lime into wedges and place them into a strong glass.

2. Add the fresh mint leaves, berries and the sugar to the glass as well and use a cocktail muddler or wooden spoon to smash the mint together with the sugar and limes. This process helps the mint leaves, berries and the lime to release their natural oils and juices.

3. Add about half a cup of ice cubes to the glass and then pour the white rum over the top. Stir the mix briefly to mix

the rum into the minty lime mix and also to help dissolve the sugar.

4. Add the club soda to the drink and stir once to mix everything together. You do not want to stir too much or the carbonation will come out of the soda.

5. Garnish with any extra lime slices and then enjoy!

Citrus Mojito

While mojitos are based around lime and mint, adding even more citrus fruit will bring your favorite drink to a whole new level. You will love the bright flavors that all the citrus bring to the glass and how the drink is just so subtly better than when it is made with just lime.

Active Time: 5 minutes

Cooking Time: 0 Minutes

Yield: 1 glass

Ingredients:

- 10 mint leaves, fresh
- 5 teaspoons granulated sugar
- 1 ½ ounces of your favorite white rum
- 2 lime wedges
- 1 orange wedge
- 1 lemon wedge
- ½ cup fresh club soda (still bubbly)
- Ice

Directions:

1. Place the citrus wedges in a tall glass

2. Add the fresh mint leaves and the sugar to the glass as well and use a cocktail muddler or wooden spoon to smash the mint together with the sugar and citrus. This process helps the mint leaves and the fruits to release their natural oils and juices.

3. Add about half a cup of ice cubes to the glass and then pour the white rum over the top. Stir the mix briefly to mix the rum into the minty citrus mix and also to help dissolve the sugar.

4. Add the club soda to the drink and stir once to mix everything together. You do not want to stir too much or the carbonation will come out of the soda.

5. Garnish with any extra lime slices and then enjoy!

Orange Mojito

This mojito eliminates the traditional lime and adds some delicious orange. This mojito is naturally a little sweeter than one made with lime juice so there is less sugar added in- even better!

Active Time: 5 minutes

Cooking Time: 0 Minutes

Yield: 1 glass

Ingredients:

- 10 mint leaves, fresh
- 3 teaspoons granulated sugar
- 1 ½ ounces of your favorite white rum
- ½ large orange
- ½ cup fresh club soda (still bubbly)
- Ice

Directions:

1. Cut the orange into wedges and place them into a strong glass.

2. Add the fresh mint leaves, raspberries and the sugar to the glass as well and use a cocktail muddler or wooden spoon to smash the mint together with the sugar and oranges. This process helps the mint leaves and the orange to release their natural oils and juices.

3. Add about half a cup of ice cubes to the glass and then pour the white rum over the top. Stir the mix briefly to mix the rum into the minty orange mix and also to help dissolve the sugar.

4. Add the club soda to the drink and stir once to mix everything together. You do not want to stir too much or the carbonation will come out of the soda.

5. Garnish with any extra orange slices and then enjoy!

Southern Style Mojito

Sweet tea is a southern tradition and it is a natural fit for a mojito. A little sweet tea makes this classic drink even sweeter and even better!

Active Time: 5 minutes

Cooking Time: 0 Minutes

Yield: 1 glass

Ingredients:

- 10 mint leaves, fresh
- 5 teaspoons granulated sugar
- 1 ½ ounces of your favorite white rum

- ½ large lime
- ¼ cup fresh club soda (still bubbly)
- ½ cup sweet tea
- Ice

Directions:

1. Cut the half of lime into wedges and place them into a strong glass.

2. Add the fresh mint leaves and the sugar to the glass as well and use a cocktail muddler or wooden spoon to smash the mint together with the sugar and limes. This process helps the mint leaves and the lime to release their natural oils and juices.

3. Add about half a cup of ice cubes to the glass and then pour the white rum over the top. Stir the mix briefly to mix the rum into the minty lime mix and also to help dissolve the sugar.

4. Add the club soda and sweet tea to the drink and stir once to mix everything together. You do not want to stir too much or the carbonation will come out of the soda.

5. Garnish with any extra lime slices and then enjoy!

Simple, Fast Mojito

If you need to whip up a good mojito quickly, opt to use some easy to find ingredients that will lessen your work load. All you need to do to make this mojito is mix everything together and enjoy!

Active Time: 1 minutes

Cooking Time: 0 Minutes

Yield: 1 glass

Ingredients:

- 1 cup limeade
- 1 ½ ounces of your favorite white rum
- ½ cup fresh club soda (still bubbly)
- Ice

Directions:

1. Mix all the ingredients together in a glass and enjoy! Garnish with fresh mint if you have it on hand.

Mango Mojito

Not only is this drink totally delicious but it also is just fun to say- mango mojito definitely has a nice ring to it! Mango adds a nice tropical flavor to the mojito and a beautiful orange color that you won't be able to resist.

Active Time: 5 minutes

Cooking Time: 0 Minutes

Yield: 1 glass

Ingredients:

- 10 mint leaves, fresh
- 3 teaspoons granulated sugar
- 1 ½ ounces of your favorite white rum
- ½ large lime
- ½ cup cubed fresh mango
- ½ cup fresh club soda (still bubbly)
- Ice

Directions:

1. Cut the half of lime into wedges and place them into a strong glass.

2. Add the fresh mint leaves, mango and the sugar to the glass as well and use a cocktail muddler or wooden spoon to smash the mint together with the sugar and limes. This process helps the mint leaves and the lime to release their natural oils and juices.

3. Add about half a cup of ice cubes to the glass and then pour the white rum over the top. Stir the mix briefly to mix the rum into the minty lime mix and also to help dissolve the sugar.

4. Add the club soda to the drink and stir once to mix everything together. You do not want to stir too much or the carbonation will come out of the soda.

5. Garnish with any extra lime slices and then enjoy!

Caramelized Pineapple Mojito

Pineapple is great on its own but when you take the time to grill it, it will have a great caramel flavor that adds so much to your drink. Grill a little extra to enjoy as a snack on the side.

Active Time: 15 minutes

Cooking Time: 10 Minutes

Yield: 1 glass

Ingredients:

- 10 mint leaves, fresh
- 4 teaspoons granulated sugar
- 1 ½ ounces of your favorite white rum
- ½ large lime
- 2 pineapple rings
- ½ cup fresh club soda (still bubbly)
- Ice

Directions:

1. Place the pineapple rings on a preheated grill and sear each side for about 3-5 minutes to caramelize. Set aside.

2. Cut the half of lime into wedges and place them into a strong glass.

3. Add the fresh mint leaves, half the pineapple and the sugar to the glass as well and use a cocktail muddler or wooden spoon to smash the mint together with the sugar and limes. This process helps the mint leaves and the lime to release their natural oils and juices.

4. Add about half a cup of ice cubes to the glass and then pour the white rum over the top. Stir the mix briefly to mix

the rum into the minty lime mix and also to help dissolve the sugar.

5. Add the club soda to the drink and stir once to mix everything together. You do not want to stir too much or the carbonation will come out of the soda.

6. Garnish with the extra pineapple slice and enjoy!

Passionfruit Mojito

Passionfruit is an amazing fruit that does not get used enough. Find fresh passionfruit to make this drink even more incredible but look for passionfruit puree in the freezer section of your grocery store as well.

Active Time: 5 minutes

Cooking Time: 0 Minutes

Yield: 1 glass

Ingredients:

- 10 mint leaves, fresh
- 5 teaspoons granulated sugar
- 1 ½ ounces of your favorite white rum
- ½ large lime
- ½ passionfruit (or ¼ cup passionfruit puree)
- ½ cup fresh club soda (still bubbly)
- Ice

Directions:

1. Cut the half of lime into wedges and place them into a strong glass.

2. Add the fresh mint leaves, passionfruit and the sugar to the glass as well and use a cocktail muddler or wooden spoon to smash the mint together with the sugar and limes. This process helps the mint leaves and the lime to release their natural oils and juices.

3. Add about half a cup of ice cubes to the glass and then pour the white rum over the top. Stir the mix briefly to mix the rum into the minty lime mix and also to help dissolve the sugar.

4. Add the club soda to the drink and stir once to mix everything together. You do not want to stir too much or the carbonation will come out of the soda.

5. Garnish with any extra lime slices and then enjoy!

Blood Orange Mojito

This drink has to be one of the prettiest drinks around and also one of the most delicious.

Active Time: 5 minutes

Cooking Time: 0 Minutes

Yield: 1 glass

Ingredients:

- 10 mint leaves, fresh
- 5 teaspoons granulated sugar
- 1 ½ ounces of your favorite white rum
- 2 lime wedges
- ½ blood orange, seeds removed
- ½ cup fresh club soda (still bubbly)
- Ice

Directions:

1. Cut the blood orange into wedges and place them into a strong glass along with the lime wedges.

2. Add the fresh mint leaves and the sugar to the glass as well and use a cocktail muddler or wooden spoon to smash the mint together with the sugar and lime and oranges. This process helps the mint leaves and the lime to release their natural oils and juices.

3. Add about half a cup of ice cubes to the glass and then pour the white rum over the top. Stir the mix briefly to mix the rum into the minty lime mix and also to help dissolve the sugar.

4. Add the club soda to the drink and stir once to mix everything together. You do not want to stir too much or the carbonation will come out of the soda.

5. Garnish with any extra lime slices and then enjoy!

Watermelon Mojito

Have you ever had watermelon paired with mint? It is so revitalizing that you should definitely make it a priority to try it right away. Why not give it a try in this perfectly crafted drink? It is a total win!

Active Time: 5 minutes

Cooking Time: 0 Minutes

Yield: 1 glass

Ingredients:

- 10 mint leaves, fresh
- 5 teaspoons granulated sugar
- 1 ½ ounces of your favorite white rum
- ½ large lime
- 1 cup fresh chopped watermelon
- ¼ cup fresh club soda (still bubbly)
- Ice

Directions:

1. Cut the half of lime into wedges and place them into a strong glass.

2. Add the fresh mint leaves and the sugar to the glass as well and use a cocktail muddler or wooden spoon to smash the mint together with the sugar and limes. This process helps the mint leaves and the lime to release their natural oils and juices.

3. Add the watermelon and smash into a puree.

4. Add about half a cup of ice cubes to the glass and then pour the white rum over the top. Stir the mix briefly to mix

the rum into the minty lime mix and also to help dissolve the sugar.

5. Add the club soda to the drink and stir once to mix everything together. You do not want to stir too much or the carbonation will come out of the soda.

6. Garnish with any extra lime slices and then enjoy!

Honeydew Mojito

This drink is like green power in a glass. Honeydew is pureed to be nice and smooth, blending together perfectly with the rest of the ingredients to make a beautiful mojito.

Active Time: 10 minutes

Cooking Time: 0 Minutes

Yield: 1 glass

Ingredients:

- 1 cup chopped honeydew
- 10 mint leaves, fresh
- 5 teaspoons granulated sugar
- 1 ½ ounces of your favorite white rum
- ½ large lime
- ¼ cup fresh club soda (still bubbly)
- Ice

Directions:

1. Place the melon in a blender and puree until a smooth juice forms.

2. Cut the half of lime into wedges and place them into a strong glass.

3. Add the fresh mint leaves and the sugar to the glass as well and use a cocktail muddler or wooden spoon to smash the mint together with the sugar and limes. This process helps the mint leaves and the lime to release their natural oils and juices.

4. Add about half a cup of ice cubes to the glass and then pour the white rum over the top. Stir the mix briefly to mix

the rum into the minty lime mix and also to help dissolve the sugar.

5. Add the club soda and honeydew juice to the mix and stir once to mix everything together. You do not want to stir too much or the carbonation will come out of the soda.

6. Garnish with any extra lime slices and then enjoy!

Basil Mojito

If you are not a big fan of mint or just looking for a delicious basil based drink, this new twist on a mojito is a sure win. Skip the mint, add the basil and get a drink that is herby, flavorful and more suited for cooler weather.

Active Time: 5 minutes

Cooking Time: 0 Minutes

Yield: 1 glass

Ingredients:

- 10 fresh basil leaves
- 5 teaspoons granulated sugar
- 1 ½ ounces of your favorite white rum
- ½ large lime
- ½ cup fresh club soda (still bubbly)
- Ice

Directions:

1. Cut the half of lime into wedges and place them into a strong glass.

2. Add the fresh basil leaves and the sugar to the glass as well and use a cocktail muddler or wooden spoon to smash the mint together with the sugar and limes. This process helps the basil leaves and the lime to release their natural oils and juices.

3. Add about half a cup of ice cubes to the glass and then pour the white rum over the top. Stir the mix briefly to mix the rum into the basil lime mix and also to help dissolve the sugar.

4. Add the club soda to the drink and stir once to mix everything together. You do not want to stir too much or the carbonation will come out of the soda.

5. Garnish with any extra lime slices and then enjoy!

The Chocolate Mojito

Not only is chocolate and mint a wonderful combination but there is actually a chocolate mint plant! Cocoa powder adds an even stronger chocolate taste to make this mojito truly unique and tasty.

Active Time: 10 minutes

Cooking Time: 5 Minutes

Yield: 1 glass

Ingredients:

- 10 chocolate mint leaves, fresh
- 5 teaspoons granulated sugar
- ½ cup water
- 2 Tbsp cocoa powder
- 1 ½ ounces of your favorite white rum
- ½ cup fresh club soda (still bubbly)
- Ice

Directions:

1. Combine the sugar, water and cocoa powder in a small saucepan and bring to a boil. Stir well then let cool completely.

2. Add the fresh mint leaves and the chocolate syrup to a glass and use a cocktail muddler or wooden spoon to smash them together. This process helps the chocolate mint leaves to release their natural oils and juices.

3. Add about half a cup of ice cubes to the glass and then pour the white rum over the top. Stir the mix briefly to mix the rum into the mint mix.

4. Add the club soda to the drink and stir once to mix everything together. You do not want to stir too much or the carbonation will come out of the soda.

5. Enjoy!

Lavender Mojito

Fresh lavender has an incredibly strong taste that pairs fantastically with a mojito. This drink is like a grown up version of a classic beverage!

Active Time: 5 minutes

Cooking Time: 0 Minutes

Yield: 1 glass

Ingredients:

- 10 mint leaves, fresh
- 2 lavender springs, buds removed (culinary grade)
- 5 teaspoons granulated sugar
- 1 ½ ounces of your favorite white rum
- ½ large lime
- ½ cup fresh club soda (still bubbly)
- Ice

Directions:

1. Cut the half of lime into wedges and place them into a strong glass.

2. Add the fresh mint leaves, lavender buds and the sugar to the glass as well and use a cocktail muddler or wooden spoon to smash the mint together with the sugar and limes. This process helps the mint leaves, lavender and the lime to release their natural oils and juices.

3. Add about half a cup of ice cubes to the glass and then pour the white rum over the top. Stir the mix briefly to mix the rum into the minty lime mix and also to help dissolve the sugar.

4. Add the club soda to the drink and stir once to mix everything together. You do not want to stir too much or the carbonation will come out of the soda.

5. Garnish with any extra lime slices or lavender sprig and then enjoy!

Kombucha Mojito

Interested in making your mojito a little bit healthier? Give this drink recipe a try! Rather than using the traditional club soda, you will use kombucha which is known to have lots of health benefits.

Active Time: 5 minutes

Cooking Time: 0 Minutes

Yield: 1 glass

Ingredients:

- 10 mint leaves, fresh
- 5 teaspoons granulated sugar

- 1 ½ ounces of your favorite white rum
- ½ large lime
- ½ cup fresh kombucha (still bubbly)
- Ice

Directions:

1. Cut the half of lime into wedges and place them into a strong glass.

2. Add the fresh mint leaves and the sugar to the glass as well and use a cocktail muddler or wooden spoon to smash the mint together with the sugar and limes. This process helps the mint leaves and the lime to release their natural oils and juices.

3. Add about half a cup of ice cubes to the glass and then pour the white rum over the top. Stir the mix briefly to mix the rum into the minty lime mix and also to help dissolve the sugar.

4. Add the kombucha to the drink and stir once to mix everything together. You do not want to stir too much or the carbonation will come out of the kombucha.

5. Garnish with any extra lime slices and then enjoy!

Spicy Jalapeno Mojito

Do you like a little spice in your drink? Because this mojito recipe is spicy yet refreshing, cooling and delicious! Get ready to enjoy a little extra kick in your glass!

Active Time: 5 minutes

Cooking Time: 0 Minutes

Yield: 1 glass

Ingredients:

- 10 mint leaves, fresh
- 5 teaspoons granulated sugar
- 1 ½ ounces of your favorite white rum
- ½ large lime
- ½ jalapeno, seeds removed, chopped
- ½ cup fresh club soda (still bubbly)
- Ice

Directions:

1. Cut the half of lime into wedges and place them into a strong glass.

2. Add the fresh mint leaves, jalapeno and the sugar to the glass as well and use a cocktail muddler or wooden spoon to smash the mint together with the sugar and limes. This process helps the mint leaves and the lime to release their natural oils and juices.

3. Add about half a cup of ice cubes to the glass and then pour the white rum over the top. Stir the mix briefly to mix the rum into the minty lime mix and also to help dissolve the sugar.

4. Add the club soda to the drink and stir once to mix everything together. You do not want to stir too much or the carbonation will come out of the soda.

5. Garnish with any extra lime slices and then enjoy!

The Classic Mojito

This recipe makes one, perfect, authentic mojito that tastes exactly how a real mojito should. If you want something truly refreshing that will quench your desire for a mojito, this is the recipe you should start with!

Active Time: 5 minutes

Cooking Time: 0 Minutes

Yield: 1 glass

Ingredients:

- 10 mint leaves, fresh
- 5 teaspoons granulated sugar
- 1 ½ ounces of your favorite white rum
- ½ large lime
- ½ cup fresh club soda (still bubbly)
- Ice

Directions:

1. Cut the half of lime into wedges and place them into a strong glass.

2. Add the fresh mint leaves and the sugar to the glass as well and use a cocktail muddler or wooden spoon to smash the mint together with the sugar and limes. This process helps the mint leaves and the lime to release their natural oils and juices.

3. Add about half a cup of ice cubes to the glass and then pour the white rum over the top. Stir the mix briefly to mix the rum into the minty lime mix and also to help dissolve the sugar.

4. Add the club soda to the drink and stir once to mix everything together. You do not want to stir too much or the carbonation will come out of the soda.

5. Garnish with any extra lime slices and then enjoy!

Champagne Mojito

A champagne mojito is like a whole new world for this classic drink. It takes it up a level as far as classiness and makes for a super fancy drink that is actually very easy to make.

Active Time: 5 minutes

Cooking Time: 0 Minutes

Yield: 1 glass

Ingredients:

- 10 mint leaves, fresh
- 5 teaspoons granulated sugar
- 1 ½ ounces of your favorite white rum
- ½ large lime
- ½ cup champagne (still bubbly)
- Ice

Directions:

1. Cut the half of lime into wedges and place them into a strong glass.

2. Add the fresh mint leaves and the sugar to the glass as well and use a cocktail muddler or wooden spoon to smash the mint together with the sugar and limes. This process helps the mint leaves and the lime to release their natural oils and juices.

3. Add about half a cup of ice cubes to the glass and then pour the white rum over the top. Stir the mix briefly to mix the rum into the minty lime mix and also to help dissolve the sugar.

4. Add the champagne to the drink and stir once to mix everything together. You do not want to stir too much or the carbonation will come out of the champagne.

5. Garnish with any extra lime slices and then enjoy!

Mimosa Mojito

Combining mimosas and mojitos is like a dream come true. This is the perfect modern brunch drink that will have everyone waking up early to grab a glass!

Active Time: 5 minutes

Cooking Time: 0 Minutes

Yield: 1 glass

Ingredients:

- 10 mint leaves, fresh
- 3 teaspoons granulated sugar
- 1 ½ ounces of your favorite white rum
- ½ large orange
- ½ cup champagne (still bubbly)
- Ice

Directions:

1. Cut the orange into wedges and place them into a strong glass.

2. Add the fresh mint leaves, raspberries and the sugar to the glass as well and use a cocktail muddler or wooden spoon to smash the mint together with the sugar and oranges. This process helps the mint leaves and the orange to release their natural oils and juices.

3. Add about half a cup of ice cubes to the glass and then pour the white rum over the top. Stir the mix briefly to mix the rum into the minty orange mix and also to help dissolve the sugar.

4. Add the champagne to the drink and stir once to mix everything together. You do not want to stir too much or the carbonation will come out of the champagne.

5. Garnish with any extra orange slices and then enjoy!

Vodka Mojito

While most mojitos are made with rum, this one has pure, strong vodka. The drink has a little bit more of a kick but is perfect for those vodka drinkers in your life!

Active Time: 5 minutes

Cooking Time: 0 Minutes

Yield: 1 glass

Ingredients:

- 10 mint leaves, fresh
- 5 teaspoons granulated sugar
- 1 ½ ounces of your favorite vodka (citrus flavored, if possible)
- ½ large lime
- ½ cup fresh club soda (still bubbly)
- Ice

Directions:

1. Cut the half of lime into wedges and place them into a strong glass.

2. Add the fresh mint leaves and the sugar to the glass as well and use a cocktail muddler or wooden spoon to smash the mint together with the sugar and limes. This process helps the mint leaves and the lime to release their natural oils and juices.

3. Add about half a cup of ice cubes to the glass and then pour the vodka over the top. Stir the mix briefly to mix the vodka into the minty lime mix and also to help dissolve the sugar.

4. Add the club soda to the drink and stir once to mix everything together. You do not want to stir too much or the carbonation will come out of the soda.

5. Garnish with any extra lime slices and then enjoy!

Mojito Mocktail

If you love the flavors of a mojito but want to skip the alcohol, then this is the perfect recipe for you. In addition, this is great for any kids who want to have a fancy drink like their parents!

Active Time: 5 minutes

Cooking Time: 0 Minutes

Yield: 1 glass

Ingredients:

- 10 mint leaves, fresh
- 5 teaspoons granulated sugar
- ½ large lime
- 1 cup fresh club soda (still bubbly)
- Ice

Directions:

1. Cut the half of lime into wedges and place them into a strong glass.

2. Add the fresh mint leaves and the sugar to the glass as well and use a cocktail muddler or wooden spoon to smash the mint together with the sugar and limes. This process helps the mint leaves and the lime to release their natural oils and juices.

3. Add about half a cup of ice cubes to the glass.

4. Add the club soda to the drink and stir once to mix everything together. You do not want to stir too much or the carbonation will come out of the soda.

5. Garnish with any extra lime slices and then enjoy!

Coconut Mojito

Coconut is a perfect addition to a mojito and it also makes the drink creamier and richer while lending a wonderful tropical taste. This is very easy to make yes still is very impressive.

Active Time: 5 minutes

Cooking Time: 0 Minutes

Yield: 1 glass

Ingredients:

- 10 mint leaves, fresh
- 1 teaspoon granulated sugar
- 1 ½ ounces of your favorite white rum
- ½ large lime
- ½ cup coconut cream, stirred well
- ½ cup fresh club soda (still bubbly)
- Ice

Directions:

1. Cut the half of lime into wedges and place them into a strong glass.

2. Add the fresh mint leaves and the sugar to the glass as well and use a cocktail muddler or wooden spoon to smash the mint together with the sugar and limes. This process helps the mint leaves and the lime to release their natural oils and juices.

3. Add about half a cup of ice cubes to the glass and then pour the white rum and coconut cream over the top. Stir the mix briefly to mix the rum into the minty lime mix and also to help dissolve the sugar.

4. Add the club soda to the drink and stir once to mix everything together. You do not want to stir too much or the carbonation will come out of the soda.

5. Garnish with any extra lime slices and then enjoy!

Cucumber Mojito

Mint is very refreshing as is lime juice. But what about cucumber? That is also an amazingly refreshing component that you can add to your mojito to take it up to the next level. Use cucumber flavored vodka if you are able to find it to make the taste even stronger.

Active Time: 5 minutes

Cooking Time: 0 Minutes

Yield: 1 glass

Ingredients:

- 10 mint leaves, fresh
- 5 teaspoons granulated sugar
- 1 ½ ounces of your favorite white rum
- ½ small cucumber, sliced
- ½ large lime
- ½ cup fresh club soda (still bubbly)
- Ice

Directions:

1. Cut the half of lime into wedges and place them into a strong glass.

2. Add the fresh mint leaves, cucumber slices and the sugar to the glass as well and use a cocktail muddler or wooden spoon to smash the mint together with the sugar and limes. This process helps the mint leaves and the lime to release their natural oils and juices.

3. Add about half a cup of ice cubes to the glass and then pour the white rum over the top. Stir the mix briefly to mix the rum into the minty lime mix and also to help dissolve the sugar.

4. Add the club soda to the drink and stir once to mix everything together. You do not want to stir too much or the carbonation will come out of the soda.

5. Garnish with any extra lime slices and then enjoy!

The Cape Cod Mojito

A Cape Codder is traditionally vodka and cranberry juice. But what if you paired that classic mix with the wonders of a mojito? You would have an amazing Cape Cod Mojito!

Active Time: 5 minutes

Cooking Time: 0 Minutes

Yield: 1 glass

Ingredients:

- 10 mint leaves, fresh
- 5 teaspoons granulated sugar
- 1 ½ ounces of your favorite vodka

- ½ large lime
- ½ cup cranberry juice
- ¼ cup fresh club soda (still bubbly)
- Ice

Directions:

1. Cut the half of lime into wedges and place them into a strong glass.

2. Add the fresh mint leaves and the sugar to the glass as well and use a cocktail muddler or wooden spoon to smash the mint together with the sugar and limes. This process helps the mint leaves and the lime to release their natural oils and juices.

3. Add about half a cup of ice cubes to the glass and then pour the vodka over the top. Stir the mix briefly to mix the rum into the minty lime mix and also to help dissolve the sugar.

4. Add the club soda and cranberry juice to the drink and stir once to mix everything together. You do not want to stir too much or the carbonation will come out of the soda.

5. Garnish with any extra lime slices and then enjoy!

Sunrise Mojito

This is the best drink you can find to start your day, especially if you are on a tropical vacation. Simple yet elegant, it will set your day off on the right foot.

Active Time: 5 minutes

Cooking Time: 0 Minutes

Yield: 1 glass

Ingredients:

- 10 mint leaves, fresh
- 5 teaspoons granulated sugar
- 1 ½ ounces of your favorite white rum
- ½ large lime
- ½ cup fresh club soda (still bubbly)
- ¼ cup orange juice
- Ice

Directions:

1. Cut the half of lime into wedges and place them into a strong glass.

2. Add the fresh mint leaves and the sugar to the glass as well and use a cocktail muddler or wooden spoon to smash the mint together with the sugar and limes. This process helps the mint leaves and the lime to release their natural oils and juices.

3. Add about half a cup of ice cubes to the glass and then pour the white rum over the top. Stir the mix briefly to mix the rum into the minty lime mix and also to help dissolve the sugar.

4. Pour the orange juice in but do not stir.

5. Add the club soda to the drink and do not stir.

6. Garnish with any extra lime slices and then enjoy!